WHO IS
TERESA NEUMANN?

by

Rev. Charles M. Carty

TAN BOOKS AND PUBLISHERS, INC.
Rockford, Illinois 61105

Nihil Obstat:
    JACOBUS BROWNE
    Censor Deputatus

Imprimi POTEST:
    ✠JACOBUS
    Episcopus Fernensis
    Die 31 Maii, 1956.

Originally published by

Fathers Rumble and Carty
Radio Replies Press, Inc.
St. Paul, Minn., U.S.A.

Complete and Unabridged

PRINTED AND BOUND IN THE UNITED STATES OF AMERICA

TAN BOOKS AND PUBLISHERS, INC.
P.O. Box 424
Rockford, Illinois 61105

1974

WHO IS TERESA NEUMANN?
by Rev. Charles Carty

When by the recéption of the stigmata and other charismata Teresa Neumann became an object of interest for the Catholics of the world, crowds from all parts flocked to see her. Many of the more important visitors obtained long interviews with her during which they questioned her much in the same way as St. Bernadette of Lourdes and the three children of Fatima had been questioned. Besides the fact that she was wearied by being made to repeat the same story almost every day, some of these verbal accounts were published coloured by the views of the respective writers. In addition, she was the object of violent attacks in the atheistic press. In these circumstances Fr. Leopold Witt, Parish Priest of the neighbouring parish of Munchenreuth, decided to write a book that would satisfy the desire of those who wanted an account of her life in her own words, give an explanation of the mystical phenomena and answer objections raised. Fr. Witt was well qualified for the task, for he was a learned man, had been a frequent visitor to Konnersreuth, and had, with the help of his sister, Dr. Leopoldine Witt, thoroughly investigated Teresa Neumann's case. He arrived on June 28th 1926, and in the presence of Fr. Naber, Parish Priest of Konnersreuth, got Teresa to tell the story of her life from her earliest youth in her own words. This he wrote down verbatim. The task took him two days, on the first of which he spent five hours writing, and on the second, seven hours. The scope of this pamphlet does not permit of giving the account in full, but everything of importance will be given in Teresa's own words; the rest will be summarized.

Before commencing to record Teresa's story, Fr. Witt gives the following brief account of the circumstances of the Neumann family and a glimpse of her childhood.

THE NEUMANN FAMILY

"The Neumann family are simple honest folk of the small farmer class. Like thousands of similar families they live happily, contented with the necessities of life without any of its luxuries. To supplement the income of his small farm of four cows, the father plies the trade of tailor, while the mother with the help of her children does the farming. There are ten surviving children; there was another, a boy, who died in infancy.

"Although the Neumann children knew little about making money, as town children would, they had to learn early what it is to earn one's bread by hard work. Teresa, as the eldest daughter, remembers well how her mother arranged all the work. She even did the ploughing, pulling the pram along behind. Housework, washing for example, she often did at night. 'Yes,' the mother said with a smile, 'when the husband has another job, it cannot be otherwise. In spite of all the work, I have never been really ill all my life.'

"Teresa was the eldest of the family; she was born on Good Friday, April 8th 1898. Though she was the eldest child she was not spoiled; she received the same solid education as the rest of the family which, thank God, is still common in Bavaria. Such an upbringing is a blessing nothing can replace. All who know the Neumann family say: 'What the Neumanns required of the children before everything was that they should obey their parents to the letter.'"

TERESA'S EARLIEST REMINISCENCES

"If we talked in church," said Teresa with happy thoughts of her childhood, "when we came home we had to kneel on a log of wood and say the Rosary," To be sure, we can hardly imagine that Teresa ever talked in church. But children will be children and a strict father is, and should be, vigilant.

"When we were at home, if father gave us a stern look, we knew what was coming."

"When we had come back from school and had been busy in mother's absence, in kitchen or stable, we would run to meet her as she returned from the field and say proudly, 'Mother, we have done this and that.' In the evening we sat around father at the table and learned our lessons and knitted.' 'Ah! how lovely it was,' says Teresa with a happy, grateful laugh—'and father learned with us, joining in always in his own old way, as he had formerly done at school himself. During the mid-day break, we were not allowed to run about the street until school began again, but had to help with the washing-up or other odd jobs in order to lend mother a hand.'"

"Already in the last half of day school, I went to work from one o'clock in the afternoon on Fockenfield farm, a good quarter-of-an-hour's walk away and was delighted to be able to lighten my father's heavy burden with his large family with my first wages of 60 pfennig (about 6d.) for a half day's work."

"I am sometimes asked by people whether I really spent my days in prayer. No! I was accustomed to hard work from my childhood and became tall and strong, although the work was continuous and often heavy. My beloved parents tried to spare me, as I was still only a child, but let me off nothing that could be expected of me. The circumstances of life, with the discipline of all sorts of difficulties, are as plain a manifestation of what God wills for us as if an angel had brought them straight from heaven."

"When I was fourteen (1912), my parents placed me in service with Mr. Martin Neumann at Konnersreuth. Work on the land is often harder than in factories. But my parents' idea was: too much liberty is not always good for young people. Besides, the work of peasants is healthy, and after all,

3

man is born to work.

"My anxious parents did not really want to send me away from home. Had they feared that I might not stay good, they would have preferred, if at all possible, to keep me under their eyes during my period of growth. I should have preferred this myself, for I could not imagine what was to be gained by withdrawal from their kindly, though strict supervision."

"I felt so much in the right place in the Christian home of Mr. Martin Neumann that I thought no further of changing, and remained there until the accident occurred at the fire. Later, two of my sisters, Maria and Anna, were put in service with Mr. Martin Neumann."

"During the World War in 1914, our employer was called up for military service. He went to Grafenwohr and we were glad that he was not so very far away. The greater part of the responsibility rested on us three sisters then, for, besides ourselves, there was only his old father in the house, although later a small lad and a day-labourer came to work. But on Saturdays our master could often look after things again, and on occasion came home on leave. But, still, for two years the management of the establishment was on our shoulders and with it the running of the Inn attached. The man's work devolved on me as the biggest and strongest of us three. I ploughed, sowed with the drill, wheeled the manure on to the field and drove the wagon to town. I climbed up steps to the loft with sacks of grain weighing 170 lbs. At that time, during the war, we learned to our cost what work means. I was often so tired in the evening that I could hardly drag myself upstairs to bed."

As we shall see more fully at the end of this chapter, there were indications that Almighty God had designs on her soul from her earliest years. Though there is no record of her having made a vow of virginity, there is proof that she had a firm unshakable determination to remain a virgin dating back to her childhood. She never attended a dance and never allowed any young man the slightest familiarity. Once when working on the hay-loft over the barn she made a perilous jump of about twelve-feet down to the threshing-floor rather than allow a young man to touch her. It is quite possible that the trouble that manifested itself in the spine later on was due in part to this jump; at any rate, it is a proof that, like St. Maria Goretti, she thought no price too high to pay for the preservation of virginal purity. Her intention of entering a convent dates back at least to her fifteenth year. When, in spite of her declared intention of doing so, young men still persisted in pressing their suit for her hand in marriage she determined to end it once for all, and the example of St. Thomas can be quoted in defense of the measures she took: she gave one of these suitors such a castigation with the goad she used on the oxen in the plough that she was never troubled again. Her resolution to go as a missionary Sister to Africa to labour for the conversion of the Negroes was not a mere empty dream, as some books suggest, but had a definite plan behind it: she had obtained her parents consent, she was in communication with a convent with houses in Africa, and with her father's permission she was putting aside part of her wages for her dowry. The outbreak of war in 1914 put an end to her hopes of entering immediately, for her father was called up for military service and she had to help support the family. However, he encouraged her by his letters from the front, telling her that as soon as the war was over she would be free to enter the convent. As we shall see presently, Almighty God had reserved a different vocation for her—the vocation of suffering.

HOW TERESA NEUMANN'S
LIFE OF SUFFERING BEGAN

On the morning of March 10th, 1918 (the year in which Padre Pio received the stigmata) a life of suffering began for Teresa which has now lasted thirty-nine years and which has not yet ended. The Divine favours bestowed on her at the end of the first period of this suffering would suggest that the Job-like afflications that came crowding upon her in the midst of her health and strength were permitted by God (as happened in the case of many others of His servants), to serve as a preparation for the reception of the stigmata.

It was Sunday morning. Teresa had been at work since soon after five, and was fasting, as she had intended to receive Holy Communion at the 7:30 Mass. A fire broke out in the neighbourhood of her master's property and soon spread to it. We give the account of what happened in Teresa's words:

"At the first news of the fire, I was naturally alarmed. But there was no time to talk or lament. Besides, my master's premises caught fire too and we had to work together so that our united strength might keep the flames from spreading. So I had to pull myself together and I quickly recovered from my fright. At first I helped to carry water in buckets, but as I was tall and strong, I was put standing on a chair to hand up water as high as I could reach. A man above then poured the water over the parts that were alight. In doing this I got soaked through but paid no attention to it as when I was ploughing this very often happened to me. I worked at this for probably a couple of hours and yet did not feel tired out.

"In my excitement I had too much confidence in my strength. I was just about to pass up another load of water when the bucket suddenly fell out of my hands. I could not go on; I had a pain in my back as if something had snapped in me; I had to get off my chair and leave the scene of action. As I was no longer of use in helping with the fire, I felt that I would like to help in some other way and so went into the stables to feed the animals, but I was not fit for this either.

"There was nothing for me, therefore, but to go to bed. But I could not get up the stairs. Not knowing what to do, I decided to go home to mother, my parents' house being only about a hundred yards away. My mother met me with the anxious question: 'What's wrong with you? You are stooped and bent.' To this I replied: 'I don't know. My back hurts and I can hardly move. It feels just as if someone had tied a cord tightly round my body.' So mother said, 'Go to bed and perspire and then you will soon be better.' I lay down on the stone bench in the living-room. I felt a bit better and towards evening I returned to my master. I was able to go upstairs and lie down in bed. My back and all my limbs ached.

"After a couple of days I got up. I could still do only very light work. I carried on till April, dragging myself about painfully. My sister, Ottilia, had entered my master's service as a substitute. As it was the time for planting potatoes, my sister thought I might pick some seed. I went down into the cellar and tried to carry up in a sack as much as my weakened condition permitted. *I got up four or five steps but then fell down backwards into the cellar again. I could not rise but had to lie there until my sister came to see what had happened to me and the potatoes.* Then she helped me up and supported by her, I managed to leave the cellar. I could no longer eat. To be idle and out in service in a stranger's house was unbearable to me.

"One might thing that chaff-cutting is not hard work but I could not even do that and sat down exhausted. I was found

7

so by Mrs. Eckert who had just come on a visit from Munich and who said in astonishment: 'Whatever is wrong with you to make you sit down?' I said: 'I cannot go on; I have such a pain in my back.' At her suggestion I went home and stayed there in bed for a week. Father was just home on leave from the front. After my mother had seen me like this for a week, she said; "Resl, this can't go on any longer,' and sent me to the doctor at Waldsassen."

That is Teresa's own account of how she contracted the illness which lasted seven years. We shall now quote the account given by Dr. Gerlich. The man who carried out the longest and most minute investigation of the facts of the case is Dr. Gerlich, a newspaper editor from Munich who became a convert to the Catholic Church as a result of his investigations. His account of facts is accepted by all, though the minority do not accept his explanations. The following, then, is a summary of the facts of the case as given by Fr. Leopold Witt and by Dr. Gerlich in his book published in 1929:

On March 10th 1918, a fire broke out in a stable near the house of Teresa Neumann's employer. Most of the men of Konnersreuth were away at the war and so the women were called upon to help to extinguish the fire. As Teresa Neumann was acknowledged to be the strongest, she got the hardest task, which was to stand on a chair about two feet high and hand up pails of water weighing from 30 to 40 lbs. to her employer who stood above her on the wall of the stable, nine feet high. She had to bend down to receive the pails, turn round and hoist them up above her head as far as she could reach. As was natural, some of the water spilled down on her and drenched her clothes; at the same time she was covered with perspiration from the violent exercise. She continued hoisting the heavy pails for two hours and she tells us that she was not exhausted. We may well believe her, for she had been accustomed to heavy manual labour such as ploughing and harrowing, threshing and carrying heavy sacks. Suddenly she felt a sharp pain in her spine as if something had snapped and the pail dropped from her hands. She could lift no more and was obliged to go away stooping and bent to the left. She tried to mount the staircase to her room in her employer's house to change her sodden garments but was unable to do so. She then went to her own house, a few hundred yards away and complained of a violent pain in the back to her mother. From that time on, any serious exertion caused her pain and any strain on her back caused her to fall. She endeavoured to keep her employment but being no longer able to work in the fields she tried to do inside jobs. This did not last long, for when carrying up a small quantity of potatoes from a cellar she fell down the stone steps, striking the back of her head against the lowest step. Her sister found her there an hour later unconscious and bleeding from the head. She said afterwards that she felt a pain and thought that her eyes would jump out of their sockets. After that her eyes began to give trouble. There were several other falls, three of which were on the back of her head and were very severe. After each fall her sight was further impaired and her nervous system showed signs of injury. After a fall from a ladder on August 1st, she began to suffer from convulsions; a few days after another fall, which happened on October 19th she became paralysed on one side and her sight became so bad that she could hardly recognize her mother. Finally she became totally blind after a fall from her invalid chair on 17th March 1919.

The drenching with cold water on a March morning while perspiring profusely brought on lung trouble; it began with a cough, then pleurisy set in and finally she got pneumonia.

Her digestive system was affected immediately after the events of March 10th. First there was vomiting and distaste for food, then the nervous system of the abdomen was deranged; this continued for six years until finally she got acute appendicitis. In addition, her whole body became covered with suppurating sores that gave off a foul odour. Archbishop Teodorowicz sums up her pitiable condition as follows:

"After a short ailment of the eyes total blindness followed; never ending night surrounded poor Teresa. Abscesses formed in the ears and for some time she lost hearing. The mere act of eating became a burden to her. Her sense of touch was also affected. Even breathing brought its difficulties; these arose from the nauseating odour of the foulness of her wounds and from such shortness of breath that in her attacks she became almost blue. The suffering was greatly increased through severe contraction of the muscles; . . . . . on the left foot, deep, bleeding painful wounds formed." 'The left foot,' says Teresa herself, 'had no skin from the ankle to the sole. The ankle bone was exposed. On my back I had six or eight spots as large as a paper Mark, the width of the hand. Water, blood and matter oozed out of all the wounds.' "

Her sufferings exceeded those of Job. Job lost all his temporal possessions and became covered with sores. Teresa Neumann lost what she valued more than money, her health and strength and her hope of realizing her ambition to become a missionary Sister; she not only became covered with sores but afflicted with almost every form of disease which flesh is heir to.

During these eight years of suffering there was never the slightest sign that her mind was in any way affected. Her behaviour during these eight years was just what a person might have expected from reading the history of her early

10

years. She had not only wished, but actually arranged to become a missionary Sister; when stricken down she desired eagerly to get cured in order to follow her religious vocation; when she began to realize that her health was gone, she manifested impatience at being reduced to a life of inactivity; finally, when all hope of recovery had vanished, with the assistance of divine grace, she accepted the will of God and even came to love her life of suffering, not from a morbid desire of suffering but because by suffering she could help to win souls for God. She expresses this idea in her own words as follows:

"I resigned myself to the will of God because the duty of every Christian is to accept the cross which the Saviour sends. It would be a sin to strive against the Will of God. I did not accept the cross because of the cross, but in devotion to the cross of the Saviour . . . . . My pains by themselves are of no avail to save souls but only when united with the pains of Our Lord."[1] Later on in life she realized more fully the value of sufferings borne with patience and united to those of Christ when she said: "If it were possible I would willingly accept sufferings in heaven in order to bring more souls to the Saviour."

Attempts Made to Cure Her Ailments

Within their slender means, her parents made every possible attempt to afford her medical assistance, and when it was evident that medical skill was of no avail they continued to bestow on her the most loving attention. As soon as her mother realized that her condition was serious, she called in Dr. Göbel who was doing duty for the local doctor, Dr. Seidl, who was absent at the war. Dr. Göbel sent her to a hospital where she was treated for seven weeks, chiefly for inflammation of the stomach. As she got no relief and her mother could not afford to pay any longer, she returned home. Then her mother sent for an old doctor named Dr. Burkhart who examined her several times. There is no written record of his diagnosis but, according to Dr. Gerlich who made enquiries about it, Dr. Burkhart attributed her maladies to the injury in her spine and her blindness to the falls that injured her skull. Dr. Burkhart died in 1918. Two other doctors, Dr. Hilzelberger and Dr. Frank, were called in by Teresa's mother. The former held out some hopes of recovery, while the latter ordered complete rest. A nursing Sister from a neighbouring hospital, named Sister Regintrude, called to see her constantly. This Sister noticed two protuberances on the spine at the place where Teresa complained of the pain.

Dr. Seidl returned from the war in the spring of 1919 and was called in soon afterwards. He remained their family doctor from that time until his retirement. When he began to treat Teresa, she was already blind and paralysed. He tried every kind of treatment but failed completely to arrest the course of her various maladies. He had not seen her till more than a year after her illness began and therefore he had no first-hand information as to what was its exact cause. *In a booklet, however, which he published in 1929 he argues that there was no natural explanation for the extra-ordinary cures and the phenomena that followed them.* But that is anticipating.

At this point, what is to be noted is that all natural means of curing her infirmity that her parents could afford were taken, and that they were completely ineffective either to cure them or to arrest their progress.

The Series of Extraordinary Cures

There were six extraordinary cures in all and all of them were connected with St. Teresa of Lisieux. In the case of five of them there was an external sign which afforded an argument that St. Teresa had intervened. In the case of the sixth, which was the most sensational, there was the fact that the long-sanding disease of the lungs disappeared suddenly and Teresa's statement that a light appeared and a voice that she had heard several times previously spoke to her. Four of the cures were accompanied by prophetic utterances which have since been fulfilled. The following is the list of cures:

The first was the cure of her blindness. It occurred on April 29th, 1923, the day of Beatification of St. Teresa of Lisieux, for which intention Teresa Neumann had commenced a novena. She had been striving to imitate the virtues of the Little Flower in preparation for entering a convent, when she was stricken down with illness.

The second was the cure of the abscess on the left foot when amputation was being considered as a means of saving her leg. This occurred on May 3rd 1925 and took place almost immediately after three rose leaves from the grave of the Little Flower had been inserted under the bandages on her left foot.

The third was the cure of her paralysis and of the ulcers on her back. This occurred on May 17 1925, the day of the Canonization of St. Teresa. A bright light appeared, a voice spoke to her, and a hand grasped hers and assisted her to sit up. The voice told her that she would have much to suffer but that by suffering she could help to save many souls.

The fourth cure was the restoration of her strength so that she could walk alone. It occurred on September 30th, the anniversary of the death of St. Teresa. The voice told her to follow her confessor's direction and to keep him informed of everything. It told her also to mortify her inclinations and to remain simple and childlike.

The fifth was the cure of appendicitis. This occurred on

November 7th 1925. Dr. Seidl had diagnosed appendicitis, and arrangements had been made to take her to a hospital for an operation. With the permission of Fr. Naber, who was present, she appealed to St. Teresa for help and applied a relic to the place where she felt the pain. She was cured immediately. Dr. Seidl affirmed on oath afterwards that it was really a case of appendicitis.

The sixth and last in order of time, which occurred on November 19th 1926, was the cure of her long-standing lung trouble. Pneumonia had at last set in and her life was despaired of. Fr. Naber had administered the last Sacraments and ordered the blessed candle to be put in her hand in preparation for death. He had previously asked the bystanders to pray to St. Teresa of Lisieux for her. Just at the moment when she seemed to be about to expire she suddenly sat up perfectly cured. The Voice again spoke to her, told her that the Saviour was pleased with her resignation; that her cure was granted for the sake of others, and that she must suffer more and so cooperate with priests in the salvation of souls.

Another sudden cure, which also has been attributed to St. Teresa of Lisieux for the reason that, when it happened, the familiar voice spoke to her, occurred some time before the cure of the pneumonia, but it has not been included in the above list because the illness from which she was cured was not connected with the events of March 10th 1918.

The following are the natural conclusions from the above statement of facts:—

(1)   There were external physical causes—over-exertion, drenching with water while in a surfeit, severe falls on the back of the head—for the various maladies.

(2)   The various maladies—blindness, paralysis, suppurating sores, appendicitis, pneumonia—had reached an extreme

14

stage when the cures occurred.

(3) Five of the cures were connected with St. Teresa of Lisieux through an external circumstance: two of them occurred after relics of St. Teresa had been applied, the other three on days of devotion to St. Teresa.

The subsequent history of Teresa Neumann's case for the past forty-three years helps to confirm these conclusions. The prophecy made and recorded at the time, that she was to have further suffering and that no doctor would be able to help her has been fulfilled. The time of the cures syn-' chronises with the reception of the stigmata and other remarkable favours: most of the cures occurred shortly before receiving the stigmata and the last in the November after she had received them. It was fitting that she should have been cured of her maladies before she got the stigmata lest these might be attributed to some bodily defect. Besides, the granting of the stigmata can be interpreted as a sign that God was pleased with her patient submission to His holy Will and a further proof that the cures were not due to natural causes but to His divine power through the instrumentality of St. Teresa.

Bed Sores

"I was extremely glad that from Epiphany 1923, I was at least able to receive Holy Communion. In *thanksgiving, I offered to God the sufferings and pain of that time.* They were increased to a considerable extent by the violent contraction of the muscles. The left foot was quite contorted; it had shrunk up under the lower end of the right thigh. The left sole stood out so far sideways that it had to have its own covering. Thus the right leg always lay on the left one. Because of this pressure, such a dreadful sore developed on the

15

left foot that mother began to fear that it might have to be amputated. *There was no skin left from ankle to toe, the bone was bare.* On the back I had six or eight bed sores the size of a shilling or even a hand's breadth. From all these wounds, water, blood and matter oozed. No one knows better than my good mother who had to nurse me with Zenzl how trying the putrid smell of these sores could be. The best treatment was with the fat of fowls, and good folk brought this in such quantities that we were never without it."

Recovery from Blindness

"It was six o'clock on the morning of 29th April 1925. My father was going to take a short journey on my behalf and came to my bedside saying, 'Resl, I'm going now.' I was awake but saw nothing of my father standing there. He went off in the direction of Mitterteich to the railway.

"About half an hour afterwards, I suddenly opened my eyes. I saw my hands and my white bed jacket. Was I dreaming? I rubbed my eyes and looked about me. I saw the pictures of saints on the wall and gazed at them as at dear, old acquaintances from whom I had long been parted.

"Then a woman came into the room. I did not know who it was. 'Who are you?' I asked in astonishment. To my question she gave a surprised reply. Then I knew her by her voice; it was my sister Zenzl. During the four years in which I had not seen her, she had grown up quite a lot, and so I had not been able to recognize her.

"She ran out quickly and called my mother. She came upstairs and I recognized her at once as she had not changed. I greeted her in rapture, 'Mother, I can see!' My mother was stunned by this news and could hardly believe it. 'Resl, you are dreaming!' With trembling hands she held up a flower before my eyes, for I always took a special delight in flowers.

I reached for the white flower. My mother still could not be-lieve and held up another. I stretched out my hand for the red flower thinking, these flowers would do nicely for church.

"My sister, Ottilia was with my former employer. Mother sent Zenzl to her, but called after her, 'Don't tell him in case it isn't true!' When Ottilia came, I was surprised and said, 'How tall you have grown during this time!' We both cried together. In the course of the afternoon, a number of my friends called. They were all astonished and cried and laughed together for joy.

"In the evening father returned. I recognized him at once, although it struck me that his hair had become quite grey, but I said nothing about this.

"For four years and one month I had not had the use of my eyes. Previously I had taken sight for granted; otherwise why should we have eyes in our heads? But now I realised that sight is one of God's most marvellous gifts for which we should thank Him every day. Now and again some people are deprived of this precious gift of God; why, God alone knows. All the more, then, should others realise how truly everything is the gift of God alone, Who, in the mighty achievement of the marvels of His divine creation, called into being the whole world and everything in heaven and earth."

At this point Teresa tells how devotion to St. Teresa of Lisieux was introduced into the Neumann family, and then gives an account of her own spiritual life.

"Devotion to St. Teresa of the Child Jesus had begun in our family in 1914. In that year, soon after the outbreak of war, my father had to join the army. We were all very anxious about him. Once when he came back from Waldsassen just before going off, he had on him two small pictures of St. Teresa of the Child Jesus. I at once asked him to give me one. A small portrait of this beloved Saint hangs over my bed and

17

I link my devotion to her especially with it.

"So I had recovered my eyesight and for this I thanked God with all my heart! I was so happy about this so unexpected favour that I could not wish for anything else. Naturally, I knew and had just had personal experience of the fact, that God is infinitely good, far beyond our feeble comprehension, and, often even beyond all our expectation. If, from the beginning, God had decided to wait for us, we should indeed have been the losers."

Devotions of her early life

"When I am downstairs among the family or upstairs in my room and I hear the others praying I join in, using the prayers learnt at home or at school. As a morning prayer I say, 'To Thee, I awake, dear Lord,' and at night, 'Before I betake myself to rest.' In addition, I always say a few Our Fathers for the Holy Souls. Especially when I was so ill and in my weakness often could not pray myself, I found what a blessing it is when we can join with others.

"While still at Sunday School, I was accustomed to give a special intention to each day of the week. On Mondays, I pray to the Holy Ghost for all religious and those in Holy Orders. On Tuesdays, I honour the Holy Innocents and the Holy Angels, and I pray for children. On Wednesdays, I pray to St. Joseph and commend to him families and Christian associations, as well as those who must work all day. On Thursdays, I pray to Jesus in the most Holy Sacrament of the altar and for all those who consecrate and distribute It, priests, especially missionaries who, either at home or in pagan countries, work for the conversion of souls. On Fridays, I honour the bitter Passion and Death of Jesus Christ and the Sacred Heart of Jesus, the only begotten Son of the Eternal Father. Besides, I pray for all the suffering, sick, and dy-

18

ing, and for the poor souls in Purgatory. Saturday is dedicated to the honour of the holy Mother of God and to prayer for virgins. On Sundays, with the whole Church, I invoke the most Holy Trinity and pray for the whole world. The needs all the countless myriads of mankind are immeasurable and great beyond all, and we can, and certainly ought, according to the Will of God, to come to the help of one another.

"My chief devotion is that to the Holy Trinity. In the church there always used to hang a picture of the Holy Family of Nazareth with the Eternal Father and the Holy Ghost. This picture had become old and worn. Once I had some money, but what is the use of money to me, I need nothing; so I bought a new picture and hung it up in church instead of the old one. I always go to this picture and decorate it with fresh flowers whenever I visit the church.

"Whenever I go into church, the first thing I do is to ask the Eternal Father that I may know the Will of God and that it may be accomplished in me. Then I ask the Holy Ghost to let me know, throughout the day, how I can please the Eternal Father. Of course, one often resolves to do something good and then does not do it; I therefore always commend mine to God. Then I ask the Child Jesus for all the virtues that are necessary for us to follow our divine Saviour. Then I turn to the Mother of God and ask her for meekness and purity. I ask St. Joseph to give me modesty and zeal in the fulfillment of the duties of my state in life, and pray especially for the fathers of families.

"I pray much for the conversion of pood sinners and for those individuals among them who, I think, need it most. Yet most of them do not know this. Sometimes a person comes and askes me to include him in my prayers so that he may return to the right path. Then I like to say, 'Let us pray for one another.' Not only we can but must all pray for one another, and there is nothing that pleases God more. Sometimes one goes, just as he has come, out into the wide world on a way known to God but I lose sight of him. But the eyes of God follow all men step by step and every one knows how to find God in his own time.

"At Holy Mass I follow the German Missal. I was led to do this by my edition of *'Imitation of Christ'* in which there is a chapter at the beginning entitled: Holy Mass as said by the Priest at the Altar. I began that when I was in Sunday School."

Cure of running sore on her left foot

"The incessant flow of matter from my left foot was always a cause of anxiety for my mother. She began to fear that it might have to be amputated. The discharge had lasted for six months without there being the slightest sign of improvement. So I thought it would not be in any way contrary to the Will of God if I asked for at least a slight alleviation of this evil. Although the power of God is boundless, I did not ask for a complete cure; but I should have been pleased with some alleviation which would have eased my mother's mind a little.

"Fr. Seraphin of the Carmelite Monastery at Reichach-on-Inn had sent me some rose leaves from St. Teresa's grave.

"One evening, my sister Zenzl had bound up my foot again. The next evening we pushed the rose leaves under the bandage. I did not notice any immediate change. After a few minutes I felt a violent itch on the diseased spot and then the pain was gone. I asked my sister to remove the bandage but she had not the time and did not think that the dressing should be renewed. So I had to be patient until the next evening.

"When we removed the bandage, we found that it was

stuck to the sheet with blood and pus. I had not been able to move my leg because it was bent under. My sister looked at the foot as she undid the bandage; it had formed a new but fine skin which looked bluish. The three rose leaves were stuck in the blood and pus on the bandage and my foot was healed."

At that time neither Teresa nor her parents had any idea that this wonderful cure was only the beginning of further great benefits from little St. Teresa.

THE PARALYSIS CURED—MAY 17th 1925 THE DAY OF THE CANONIZATION OF ST. TERESA AT LISIEUX

Teresa tells how the cure occurred

"One afternoon during the May devotions, I was just saying my Rosary. While I was blind, of course, I had no other method of praying. Certainly I should have liked to go to church, but since that was not possible, I said the Rosary at home. I had just reached the second mystery, 'He ascended into heaven.' The following Thursday was Ascension Day. I was thinking, 'What must the Apostles have felt like when their Lord and Master prepared to leave them?' 'They must have felt that He was still very necessary to them.' Suddenly a light appeared before me. At first it startled me very much. It was a white light in front of me over the bed. It did my eyes good. In the first moments of surprise I gave a cry that my parents heard downstairs. They came up, my father first. I saw nothing but the white light. My father spoke to me and held up something for me to drink. I did not notice anything. I heard a voice out of the light, 'Resl, would you not

21

like to be well?' I answered 'To me all is welcome, to live or to die, to ail or be well; God knows best.' The voice asked again, 'Would you be happy if you could help yourself again?' I replied, 'I find pleasure in all that comes from God.' Then I reckoned up all that gave me pleasure, 'All flowers and the birds give me pleasure, or else fresh suffering; that gives variety. But my greatest pleasure is in our dear Saviour.' But the voice insisted, 'You must have some small joy. You can sit up, try, I will help you.' At these words, something took hold of my right hand. Mother says I stretched upwards and adds that all this time I did not look my usual self.

"When I raised myself the first time, I felt a sharp pain in my back and stretched out my hand to where the pain was. Mother says that at the same time I showed my teeth."

"The voice continued, 'But you still must suffer, much, and for a long time, and no doctor will be able to help you. But do not be afraid! I have helped you thus far and will do so still more. Only through suffering can you fulfill your vocation, which is to be a victim and so help priests. Far more souls are saved by suffering than by brilliant preaching. I have written this before.'

"Who it was and who spoke, I do not know. The voice had certainly given me no name. None of us knew who had written the last sentence. Only on the following day did the Parish Priest find it in the writings of St. Teresa of the Child Jesus, having borrowed the book, as he did not possess a copy himself. Then the voice went on, 'You can walk too.'

"The light vanished and I noticed again that I was in bed in my room. Then I cried because the light had gone away. I thought, 'How am I!' I was quite well; my back no longer hurts me."

Complete Recovery

"It was half an hour after midnight on 30th September 1925. This was the anniversary of the death of St. Teresa of the Child Jesus. I was still awake and lay in bed reading by electric light the Litany in honour of St. Teresa. I expected anything but what then took place. Suddenly a light shone before me, the same light as when I was cured of paralysis. It again came quite suddenly, as lightning does. In comparison with it, the electric light was mere darkness. This light could quite as well have come by day; then it would have outshone the sun, dimming its light. To be able to enjoy this light for a mere quarter of an hour, had I to purchase it, I would gladly give both my eyes. I saw and I looked; light, but no figure or form.

"I know of no joy I can compare with the unutterable bliss which filled me when I looked at it. When, on 29th April 1923, I was cured of my blindness of four years' duration, and my eyes for the first time saw daylight again, that was rapture for me, for even our natural sight is one of God's wonders. But the intense happiness with which I greeted my long-lost sight was nothing in comparison with this later and sublimer light.

"Then, too, I heard the voice again. It was the same that I remembered so well. I should not forget its beneficent splendour if I lived for a thousand years. The voice always speaks standard German, but addresses me with the homely 'Resl.' I answered in the simple language that we speak here.

"With what shall I compare this voice? Certainly I have never heard its like. I know nothing of music. I hear of concerts in town and how everybody flocks to them and how musical experts rave about them, as if to listen to a beautiful piece of music were like a quarter of an hour in heaven. But no one would give his eyes for it. The most beautiful music I know is that of our church choir at Konnersreuth. But it cannot produce any harmony the sweet tone of which would compete with my voice. In comparison with it any other sound is mere noise.

"The voice said, 'You can now walk without aid. The suffering that affects your eyes will be taken away. Something more painful will come instead. —Encourage people to trust in God.' 'But,' I objected, 'I do not know myself whether I am on the right track or whether I am doing everything wrong. Some say that everything to do with me is a fraud, while many are angry about me. And so I may well doubt if I am doing everything right.' Then the voice which came and went, reminded me of the remedy which all Catholics have against such doubts and qualms of conscience: 'Follow in blind obedience the advice of your Confessor and confide everything to him.' The 'ego in you should be gradually eradicated. Always remain childlike and simple.' "

"The voice was silent and the light disappeared. I again saw the usual surroundings of my room and the little prayer book with the Litany open in my hand, while the electric light shed a dim light. I did not know whether I had been dreaming; I rubbed my eyes and looked round.

"Then I rose and tried to walk. I left the stick, of which I had so far made so much use, leaning against the wall in the corner. Before, I had not been able to cross the room alone; I always had to hold on to the furniture. But now I walked about quite freely for a good quarter of an hour round the room."

It was nearly seven years since she had been able to go alone into the open air.

Appendicitis develops and is suddenly cured

Our readers will remember that among the ailments that Teresa Neumann contracted as a result of the injury to her spine and the drenching with water while covered with perspiration at the extinguishing of the fire, were severe stomach and intestinal trouble and lung trouble. She was treated in a hospital for these without success, they lingered on after the cures of blindness and paralysis and it was only when all hope of saving her life seemed to have vanished that these were cured. The first of these to come to a crisis was the stomach and intestinal trouble.

The following is Teresa's account of how the appendicitis developed and was cured:

"My greatest year of grace, 1925, was not to close without my having special suffering as a sign that God had not forgotten me. On November 7th, I felt so ill that I could hardly stand and had to go to bed. Throughout the night I was very bad. The next day I was numb with pain and in such a state of exhaustion that I could not open my eyes.

"As I became worse, my parents sent for Dr. Seidl of Waldsassen. He came at about six o'clock in the evening.

"'Well, child, how are you?' This was the friendly way in which the family doctor we had had so many years greeted me, as he came to my bedside. Soon he added sympathetically, 'This time you really are bad.' After examining me, he said to me very decidedly, 'You have inflammation of the appendix in the highest degree.'

"Dr. Seidl, therefore decided that I must be taken at once to the hospital at Waldsassen to be operated on. He would not take the responsibility of putting it off until the next morning. He would have preferred to take me at once in his car. 'But,' he said, 'you are too weak and could not sit so long.' My poor parents were quite bewildered by this fresh misfortune. . . . . They sought a consultation with the Parish Priest in the hope that, on account of my great weakness he might, perhaps, dissuade the doctor from having me taken to the hospital, for, if the matter were indeed so serious, I might just as well die at home. He discussed it with Dr. Seidl and then gave his opinion. My parents were to recognise the Will of God in the judgment of the doctor. Then my father hastened to fetch a vehicle and my mother hurriedly prepared a bed and the linen necessary. The doctor went on to another patient and then drove to the hospital to get everything ready for an immediate operation. All this commotion lasted about half an hour.

"I was quite resigned to go, but my mother's inconsolable grief cut me to the heart. Would it be wrong of me in my distress, when all human aid had already been exhausted, to call on my great 'helper?' She herself had already promised, 'I will help you in the future, too.'

"But before I turned to little St. Teresa for help, I wished to ask the Parish Priest, so that it should not look as if I wanted to tempt God. Dr. Seidl very aptly remarked, 'St. Teresa has always had to work miracles for you.' And I said, 'I was certain that St. Teresa would help me, if I asked her.'

"The Parish Priest permitted me to ask St. Teresa to cure me without an operation if it were pleasing to God.

"Among my most treasured possessions was a relic—one hair of St. Teresa of the Child Jesus. The Carmelite Father Seraphin of Reischach sent it to me as a gift. This hair of the little Saint, so dear to me, I usually wear in a small case on a string around my neck.

"I now had this relic produced. All present began to pray aloud together to St. Teresa.

26

"Because of pain, I myself could not join in with the others, but mentally I prayed simply, saying that for myself I was quite resigned; but I besought her to listen to mother in her distress. Being feverish and weak I could manage no more, but Our dear Lord thinks more of our intention than of what we say.

"A hand appeared to me and I wanted to take hold of it but I was not able to do so. It was a white, slender hand, as Teresa's is represented in her pictures. The first three fingers were stretched out, the others closed.

"Your total surrender and cheerfulness in suffering rejoices us. *That the world may know that there is a higher power that can intervene, you will not need to be operated upon.* You are to get up and go to church, at once, *at once,* to thank God. You still have much to suffer, but you need not fear, not even inwardly. Only thus can you co-operate in the salvation of souls. You must, however, more and more mortify your own 'self.' Always remain simple as a child."

Those who criticize Fr. Naber and the little party who went with him to the Church at midnight in obedience to an unknown Voice and accuse them of credulity should remember that this was not the first time that Teresa heard the Voice, and that her hearing of the Voice had been always connected with remarkable cures for which no satisfactory natural explanation has ever been given. They should remember also that Teresa had suffered for seven years from intestinal trouble, that she had been seriously ill in bed with high fever for three days before the doctor was summoned, and that Dr. Seidl who diagnosed appendicitis was a specialist in that department.

How the last of Teresa's illness dissappeared

At this point we shall anticipate in order to give an account of the disappearance of the last of the illnesses that can be attributed to the strain and exhaustion suffered in helping to extinguish the fire in March, 1916.

It will be remembered that on that occasion she was bathed in perspiration, and at the same time her clothes became soaked through with water that dripped down from the buckets as she handed them up to the man above her. Her lungs became affected, pleurisy was soon diagnosed by her doctor and the lung trouble continued for eight years until the crisis about to be described occurred.

The crisis occurred on November 19th 1926. In the preceding Lent she had received the stigmata of the Five Wounds during a vision of the Passion and after that she had a vision of the Passion every week, except during Paschal time, from 11:00 p.m. on Thursday night to 1:00 p.m. on Friday. The crisis did not occur without warning, for Fr. Witt tells us that several weeks before November 19th she was so ill that the doctor forbade all visits. He declared that inflammation of the lungs was beginning.

Just before 11 p.m. on Thursday night, the time that the Passion ecstasy was due to begin, she was seized with a violent fit of coughing but as soon as the ecstasy began at 11 p.m. the coughing suddenly stopped and did not start again until the fourteen hours Passion ended at 1:00 p.m. on Friday. During this particular Passion ecstasy Teresa received the stigmata of the Crown of Thorns.

Fr. Witt describes what happened as follows:—

"Friday, 19th November, 1926, was so far Teresa's heaviest day of her whole suffering. On this day she was in a death agony which at about 6 p.m. made all bystanders, including

Fr. Naber, fear that each breath would be her last.

"The morning hours, and especially noon, when on this Friday Teresa saw as usual the Passion of Our Lord, were usually severe and were marked by the appearance of quite new suffering. The marks of the crown of thorns on her became visible for everyone.

"Towards evening, Teresa's condition was worse than ever. She had not enough strength to hold up her hand: her sister had to support her head. About 6 p.m. the colour of her face was pale like that of a dying person. Her lips were swollen. Her sad eyes, half open, were raised upwards, her face drooped and her nose became pointed. When she was called by her name, no matter how loudly, she gave no sign. She breathed slowly and with difficulty. Her father said, 'Her feet were already cold,' and added, weeping, 'If only her mother were here!'

"Several of Teresa's friends had also come but stood just as helpless as her relatives at the piteous sight of the sick woman. They wept, and prayed, 'St. Teresa, help us for one day more, at least until her mother comes home, if it really must be so!' Fr. Naber urged those present to pray to St. Teresa of the Child Jesus. But at last, he felt that he must admit that Teresa could not last much longer. He ordered the father to bring quickly a blessed candle (for the dying) and this was put into Teresa's hand, the top being held by one of Teresa's sisters; in the other hand, the Parish Priest placed the Crucifix of the dying. Everyone thought that each moment would be the last, and after each gasp feared the breathing would stop. Fr. Naber, together with Fr. Weber, Curate of Konnersreuth, then began to say the prayers for the dying: 'Go forth, Christian soul, etc.' The mother, who was still far away and knew nothing of what was happening, would only find the corpse of her daughter when she returned.

Teresa lay perfectly motionless.

"All of a sudden, Teresa let the candle and crucifix fall from her hands, sat up straight, stretched out her arms as in her ecstasies, and a glad, happy smile spread over her features.

"The sister, who held Teresa in her arms, was frightened by this unexpected issue and sudden accession of strength and asked herself wonderingly, 'Is this perhaps her last smile because little St. Teresa is coming to fetch her and then she will lie down and all will be over with her.' But as soon as Teresa sat up, the death rattle ceased. She did not lie down again but with eyes ever turned upwards—Teresa enjoyed a visitor from another, more beautiful world.

"The mysterious Light appeared again and out of the Light a Voice said, 'It gives our dear Lord pleasure that you are so resigned. You will not be permitted to die now. *But it happened to show the world that there is a Higher Power.* You must suffer more and co-operate with priests for the salvation of souls.' While Teresa was speaking, the others, listening interestedly, smiled with happiness. With special pleasure they followed Teresa's account, her words coming awkwardly because of her earnestness. Then sooner than usual after similar events, during which she had been living in another world, she returned with some difficulty to ordinary speech. She spoke in isolated phrases and stammeringly, like children just learning to speak.

"The next day, Teresa could get up. She had got through this difficult Friday, too, no more upset than by any other Friday.

"The wounds of the stigmata in the head remained, yet they closed the next week, as did those in the hands and feet, too. The wounds in the head open beforehand on Fridays and her white head-dress gets stained with blood all around."

STIGMATISATION

Teresa Neumann did not receive all the stigmata at the same time. She received the marks of the Five Wounds during the Lent of 1926; the marks of the Crown of Thorns, of the shoulder wound and of the scourging at later dates.

She herself gave the following account of how she received the stigmata of the Five Wounds to Fr. Leopold Witt in the presence of Fr. Naber on June 26th 1926.

"In mid-Lent 1926, the wound in my side appeared. One night I was lying still in bed. I do not know what I was actually thinking of.

"Pious thoughts may exert a great influence on a person. But in my case I was in no way aware that the wound in my side had arisen as a result of any inner effort of the soul on my part. I was not then thinking of the Wound in the side of Jesus or of a similar wound in myself. I had never seen stigmata and did not know how to imagine such a thing.

"As I lay thus in bed without thinking of anything in particular that I can expressly remember, *all at once I saw our Saviour in front of me.*

"I saw Him on the Mount of Olives. Then, as this was the first time this had happened to me, I had no idea that it had any special significance. But I saw our Saviour as He knelt there. I saw everything else clearly, the trees, the grass and the rocks, just as in a garden. I saw the three Apostles too, not lying down as generally represented, but rather seated leaning against a rock and quite listless.

"I saw our Saviour quite alone; no angel with a chalice or anybody else.

"Suddenly, while I was looking at Him, I felt such a pain in my side that I thought I was going to die. At the same

31

time, I felt as though something hot were running down me. It was blood; blood flowed continuously until noon the following day. From Friday afternoon on, the week following was quiet.

"The whole time, I was so weak that I hardly knew where I was. On Thursday, I did not even know that it was that day.

"In the second week, on the Thursday-Friday night, I saw Our Lord at the scourging-post. My side had begun to bleed again. I did not know it was Friday. I asked my mother, 'What day is it?' 'Friday,' she answered.

"Nothing exceptional happened until the next Friday. Then I saw Our Lord being crowned with thorns. My side was bleeding again.

"The Friday before Holy Week, I saw Our Saviour carrying His cross. Again my side was bleeding.

"On Maundy Thursday I saw Our Lord again on the Mount of Olives.

"My parents had not noticed what had happened to me. I succeeded in hiding from them the wound in my side (I had not yet received the other wounds) until Maundy Thursday.

Discovery of the Stigmata by her Parents

"My most faithful ally had so far been my sister Zenzl. I could rely absolutely on her for not telling anyone. So I now said to her, 'You know how anxious Mother is when anything is the matter. Wash me all over without her seeing.' My sister quickly complied, without annoying me with a lot of questions about it all.

"To make the blood-stains a little less noticeable, I wore a large black shawl round my shoulders. My parents just thought that this was on account of the cold. One day my mother told me I ought not to wear the black shawl, saying: 'You look an old grandmother in it,' and took it away. But I begged so earnestly for it that she gave it back the next day.

"Finally, on Maundy Thursday, my father asked what was wrong with me. Again I saw Our Saviour on the Mount of Olives, and by evening my side was again bleeding. My father happened to see me take off a dressing once and I asked him for another piece. When he gave me this, I asked him for a larger one. He noticed how carefully I folded it in eight and then tucked it down out of sight. I tried to hide the old piece from him in the bed. I was rather helpless in my weak state and my father noticed it all the same. And so the secret I had so carefully tried to keep was discovered. He found the linen soaked with blood and showed it to my mother. Thus, on Maundy Thursday, my parents knew of the strange haemorrhage from my side, even if they did not clearly understand what it meant.

"But on Good Friday, when I was in an ecstasy and unconscious of my surroundings, the blood flowed so copiously that the linen could no longer absorb it and it soaked through my bed-jacket. Everybody, too, could see now the blood which streamed from my eyes flooding my face. Now my parents began to suspect what was the matter with me, but could scarcely believe their eyes. So far, they knew nothing of the wounds on my hands and feet, for these had appeared for the first time that day. I do not know exactly when they did come. They were simply there on Good Friday evening.

"Nor did I know beforehand that I was to have *these* wounds, too. During the vision I had no inkling of them, for then I could not think about myself, but just gazed up the whole time at Our Saviour.

"The five wounds hurt me constantly, although I have already become accustomed to pain. It is as though something is penetrating into my hands and feet. The wound in the side seems to be really one in the heart. I feel it at every word I utter. If I draw a deep breath when speaking forcibly or hurrying, I feel a stabbing pain in my heart. If I keep quiet, I don't notice this. But I suffer this pain willingly. Actually, the wounds close up during the week. The real pain lies much deeper inside. An accidental pressure on the back of my hand or the instep of my foot I feel far less than one on the palm or sole. Because of this, I cannot use any stick, nor even stand on the soles of my feet much less walk.

"The wound on my side is in a different place from where I see it on Jesus. In my case it is just above the heart where the heart beats. It is on the left side, but only slightly sideways. I am told that learned people have discussed this from every point of view, but I can only say what is, and what I see, even if others would prefer to hear what suits them."

When the stigmata appeared on Teresa's hands and feet, the Parish Priest, Fr. Naber, suggested that they be treated as ordinary wounds and had Dr. Seidl called in. Dr. Seidl applied dressings used for ordinary wounds. These, instead of having a beneficial effect, caused considerable swelling and pain so severe that they brought on fainting fits. Fr. Naber then permitted Teresa to remove the dressings, and the swellings and pain ceased. He then recalled the words spoken by the Voice announcing further suffering and saying: "No doctor will be able to help you." Fr. Naber has been criticised by Fr. Siwek, S.F., and a few others for giving permission to Teresa to remove the dressings. Fr. Naber was in no way bound to call in a doctor to apply dressings to the stigmata; there is no Church regulation requiring any such proceeding. He would certainly have been open to criticism if he persevered in the attempt to heal the stigmata when he saw that the remedy applied was doing serious harm.

THE FURTHER HISTORY
OF TERESA'S STIGMATISATION

Fr. Leopold Witt's account brings us only to the end of the
year 1926; for the history of the development of the marks
of the Five Wounds and of the reception of the stigmata of
the shoulder wound and of the scourging we take our account
from F.X. Huber's *Das Mysterium von Konnersreuth:*

THE APPEARANCE OF THE MARKS
OF THE CROWN OF THORNS

"At the vision of the Passion on 5th November, 1926, traces
(still indistinct) of the crown of thorns stigmata became
noticeable on her head and lasting headaches followed this
new symptom of an intensification of Teresa's Passion sufferings. On Friday, 19th November, eight pronounced wounds
round her head were bleeding, drenching her white shawl with
blood. The wounds, which looked like prickings caused by
sharp thorns, have since bled at all her visions of the Passion.

"Good Friday of the following year (1927) brought a further change. *Then the wounds on her hands and feet worked
their way through from the back and instep inwards and
broke through the palms and soles. Now the wounds were
real stigmata, in form, size and formation, as actual penetra-
tions like those on the limbs of Christ on the cross; larger,
wider, gaping at back and instep, in appearance as if made
by the forcible driving in of a nail; smaller, narrower and
torn where the nail came out and entered the wood of the
cross.* Because of the continuous streaming of blood from her
eyes on this Good Friday, these were blinded, stuck together
and encrusted; the grooves of the right and left cheeks were
stiffened by the slowly coagulating blood which ran together

into the hollow of the chin and seeped on to her throat and bed-jacket.

"The side wound, too, showed a change in 1927, which appeared first on the Feast of the Sacred Heart, the left side from then on showed a gaping wound which appeared to go right through the heart. The form of the wound is worth noticing, with its edges torn up outwards as if caused by the extraction of a lance, the point of which had been thrust through.

RAYS OF LIGHT APPEAR FROM THE STIGMATA

"Rays of light have been observed by numerous witnesses, coming at times from these wounds, bright and intense, penetrating even the mittens which Teresa wore to hide and protect them. Fr. Naber had had a prie-dieu made behind the High Altar in the Parish Church so that Teresa could attend Mass without attracting the attention of the congregation while she knelt and prayed. Unfortunately this did not achieve its object at first as there was no slackening in the numbers of visits and admissions and on Sundays and Feast Days, the crowd outside was so great that the whole Choir was full of people, who even filled the space round the Altar so that Teresa was continually under observation. Several times such worshippers, either local or from a distance, had noticed with astonishment that the mark on the left hand shone as bright as the sun. Böhm, the headmaster at Konnersreuth, and Fr. Naber thought that perhaps these observations might arise from a kind of mass hallucination.

A camera, thought schoolmaster Böhm, cannot be the victim of self-deception and can have no 'hallucinations'; and so, on 17th May 1927, he placed himself amongst the worshippers behind the Altar where he had Teresa well in focus. As the 17th May was the anniversary of the Canonization of

36

Little Teresa and had already been marked by special manifestations, the possibility of something striking happening was to be reckoned with. And, in fact, the rays of light did show themselves. The schoolmaster made two exposures in order to rule out any deception. And, behold, the plates showed definitely these rays of light, which are no longer matters of debate; they are facts, observation of them is an actual sense-impression and the negatives are preserved in the episcopal archives at Regensburg.

THE MARK OF SHOULDER WOUND

"Among those in more immediate contact with Teresa Neumann, it hardly aroused any more wonder that in Lent 1929, the degree of suffering increased; she had in the meantime already experienced a notable increase in spiritual suffering. On 8th March 1929, the white bed-jacket exhibited on one shoulder an extensive blood stain—it came from a considerable wound on her shoulder which bled this day for the first time; it has since bled at all the visions of the Passion. This shoulder wound is the actual replica of that painful cut caused to Our Saviour by the heavy, sharp-edged beams he carried."

This wound on the shoulder Teresa Neumann finds to be the most painful of all the wounds; it is very large and bleeds most profusely during the vision of the carrying of the cross. It bleeds also when in her vision she sees the executioners tear off violently Our Lord's garments before the crucifixion. If it is permissible to make a deduction from this wound on Teresa Neumann's shoulder, the wound on Our Lord's shoulder must have been very painful. In revelations about the Passion made to Venerable Maria d'Agreda, Josef Menendez and others, Our Divine Lord is represented as saying that the wound on His shoulder was the most painful of all His wounds.

THE MARKS OF THE SCOURGING APPEAR

"On Good Friday, 1929, on 29th March, her nightdress and bed-jacket—which because of the copious haemorrhage had to be changed twice—showed such numerous bloodstains that an examination of her was made which showed that her body, above all her back, was covered over and over with small wounds, as from sharp brows; they were all open and bleeding. These were the marks of Christ's scourging. These, too, have since bled at the Passion ecstasies. Often there is hardly a sound spot on Teresa's body.

"This intensified bleeding is shown sometimes by the heart wound, then by the shoulder wound, then the head wounds from the thorns; the other stigmata bleed less freely. Shawl, nightgown and bed-jacket are so soaked in blood that it can almost be wrung out of them. The amount of personal and bed-linen is necessarily very large. A number of articles are, of course, preserved and documented as evidence and proof.

"Because of the stigmata, Teresa Neumann cannot tread with the whole of her foot; involuntarily she shrinks from the painful contact with the ground that the ordinary position would involve; she walks, perforce, on her heels, which is hardly surprising. By reason of the foot wound, she cannot stand or kneel for any considerable period and so the prie-dieu behind the High Altar is built for sitting or kneeling."

DESCRIPTION OF TERESA NEUMANN'S STIGMATA

Dr. Louis of Versailles visited Konnersreuth in 1930 and examined the stigmata on the hands. The following is how he describes the marks in the left hand in his booklet entitled, "Holy Week at Konnersreuth":

"On the back of the left hand I see a head of a nail, rectangular in form, slightly longer than wide in the direction of the hand. The rectangle which it forms is admirably regular and has its edges delicately adorned with zig-zag borders. It is about 15mm. by 10mm. These borders are slender and sharp like the edges of a nail forged with a hammer. The head of the nail itself is slightly arched and is round like a dome. The top of the dome itself is about two or three millimetres in thickness. It shows flat marks in several places resembling those produced by a blacksmith's hammer on a piece of iron. The colour is reddish brown like a seal of ancient wax.

"I now examine the point of the nail on the palm of the left hand. It is lying on the skin in the hollow of the hand, turned obliquely down as if by a hammer, with the point turned towards the outside of the hand. It emerges, thus bent, for a length of about 15mm. It adheres completely to the skin. It is about 4mm. in thickness and is rough and round in form. It is of the same brownish colour as the head of the nail but the cicatrice border around it is not so well defined."

This description was written in 1930. A similar description is given by F. X. Huber in his book published in 1950, with the addition that these nails were horn-like formation and that they pierced the hands and feet.

At Fr. Patrick O'Connell's visit, Fr. Naber who had before him the description by Fr. Louis, testified that the stigmata on the feet were similar to those on the hands and that they conformed to the description given by Dr. Louis. The following is a copy of what he wrote:

"Stigmata in pedibus Theresiae Neumann habent eamdem formam quam habent in manibus, i.e., habent formam clavorum sicut scripsit Dr. Louis."

Ego vidi.
NABER. parochus.

This description by Dr. Louis, shows that the stigmata of Teresa Neumann resemble very closely those of St. Francis of Assisi as described by Celano and St. Bonaventure. Fr. Thurston quotes Catholic writers who think that the description of the stigmata of St. Francis is exaggerated and he inclines to that opinion himself. We therefore give further quotation from F. X. Huber's book which corroborates the description given by Dr. Louis and show that Teresa Neumann's stigmata are really horny substances in the form of nails piercing her hands and feet—a form of stigmata for which no natural explanation has ever been attempted.

"The stigmata formed gradually; first on the backs of the hands, then in the palms; they were at first open, then the wounds became covered by a scab and surrounded by scarring. But these wounds do not bleed outside the Passion ecstasies; neither do they moisten nor discharge; outside the Friday ecstasies they are absolutely dry. They are new growths, hard and horny, around which lies an elastic, delicate membrane which breaks and bleeds during the Passion ecstasy and at the end of it closes again. (cf. Lama, Yearbook, 11-17).

"Inside, on the palm, the marks are narrower and longer. The wounds are exactly alike—something that certainly would not be so if anyone had tried to make them himself.

"The fact is to be emphasized that the wounds on the hands did not first appear where they might be expected to appear—on the palms of her hands—and so for this and many other reasons auto-suggestion as an explanation must be ruled out. They started on the backs of the hands—only later did the marks work through to the palms.

"When the stigmata do not bleed, they are covered by a fine membrane and appear sometimes a deep, dark red, sometimes fresh ruby red. According to independent medical evidence they are genuine if they arise without any artificial interference and are obtained without the taking of any action . . . .

Dr. Witz noted in 1931:

"On the back of the hands stigmata 9-11 mm. wide; in tablet-like relief raised above the surrounding skin about 2-2.5 mm., on all sides alike steeply falling edges; surface flat, but glistening.

"In the Yearbook for 1931, Ritter von Lama again gives the result of several investigations of the changes in the wounds observed at that time. These lay essentially in the fact that a sort of nail forms in the wounds and seems to consist of firm, grisly flesh; *one got the impression of a forged iron nail which goes through the hand from outside to the inside, the end of which appears to have been bent round by a hammer-blow. Between the crust in the middle of the wound and the normal skin lies a brighter edge, grooved and delicate;* and through this edge or membrane the wounds bleed. The wounds cause very little pain, only when Teresa Neumann extends her fingers, the stretching of the skin does hurt a little.

"Dr. Babor noticed the sudden outflow from the right shoulder of fresh, cherry-like blood in 1932 during the vision of the clothes being torn from Christ before the crucifixion, and in 1934 at the fifth Station (where Simon of Cyrene had to help Our Lord carry the cross) when the cross was thrust on to Our Lord's shoulder by Simon and he adds:

"'As a proof of the miraculous nature of these phenomena, nothing can be more convincing to a doctor than the remarkable way in which the times that Teresa Neumann's stigmata bleed correspond with the times of Our Divine Lord's sufferings. Thus, her hands bleed when Our Lord's hands are bound in the Garden of Gethsemani; the stigmata of the scourges bleed at 6 a.m. (8 a.m. Jerusalem time) when Our Lord was scourged; the bleeding of the wounds on her head begins soon after as she sees the Crown of Thorns placed on Our Lord's head; the shoulder wound bleeds during the vision of the carrying of the cross and again when Our Lord is stripped of His garments; and the wounds on her hands and feet bleed profusely during the vision of the crucifixion.'

"Teresa Neumann often submitted to medical examination of the heart wound—at the desire of, or with the approval of the Church—this was measured, touched, irradiated, X-rayed, described; was still oftener observed when active and bleeding; then, too when Teresa Neumann was in her Passion ecstasy, knowing nothing of what was going on around her or what was done to her, when the wound bled without her knowing, when her natural consciousness, her ordinary attention to physical happenings, when any influence by her on the process of bleeding, were completely eliminated.

"This nail-shaped formation of the wounds (occurring in past centuries in the case of some stigmatists), was something that Teresa Neumann soon noticed; with the progressive consolidation of the formation, it gave her the feeling 'as if something was pricking in the stigmata.'

"Outside the period of the Passion ecstacy these formations feel hard, almost horny; and yet are most sensitive; just at the beginning of the Passion ecstasy from Thursday evening on, they become soft and super-sensitive like fresh wounds."

There is a general impression that when St. Francis of Assisi received the stigmata, he received them in perfect form, and that afterwards there was no change or development. This is by no means certain, for St. Bonaventure describes his stigmatisation as follows:

"When the vision disappeared, it left a most marvellous ardour in his heart, and it impressed on his flesh a no less wonderful image of the signs which he had seen. For immediately the marks *of the nails began to appear* in his hands

42

and feet as he had seen a little before on the image of the Crucified Man. The right side also appeared as if pierced by a lance and was covered by a red cicatrice." (*Vita St. Francisi* by St. Bonaventure).

It is to be noted that St. Bonaventure does not say that the marks of the nails "appeared," but "began to appear." Therefore those few who contend that true stigmata should appear perfect and complete when first bestowed and that there should be no change or development cannot quote the case of St. Francis in support of their contention.

Though there has been development in Teresa Neumann's stigmata as most probably there was in the cases of other stigmatists, with the exception of the marks of the Crown of Thorns, there has been no change since 1930 when they had become completely developed. The stigmata of the Crown of Thorns originally consisted of eight wounds. In this year (1953) six additional marks have appeared on her head. In the book by Dr. Roy and Fr. Joyce, a prophecy of Teresa's is recorded which says that when the marks of the Crown of Thorns form a circle around her forehead it will be a sign of her death, and that when she dies she will come for Fr. Naber.

THE BLEEDING

Eye-Witnesses testify to the Reality of the Bleeding of the Stigmata

"In his article *The Living Replica of the Crucified,* which appeared in Czech in 1928, Dr. Hynek declares: (p. 70) 'On Good Friday morning, 1928, for eight to ten minutes, I was able to observe at close quarters the bleeding of the stigma on the back of her left hand; without any doubt one could see fresh, red human blood flow from the small aperture . . . in such quantity that it could have made a band a finger wide around her wrist.' This was at his third visit to Konnersreuth, in the presence of Mgr. Doskocil of Konigsgrätz. 'That these (wounds) in spite of bleeding neither scar over nor inflame, but remain quite intact, is an especially hard nut for doubters to crack, and can in no way be explained.' (Hynek, p. 10). 'When one had observed for some minutes the uninterrupted flow of blood, one feels that it cannot be caused by any swindle. An experienced surgeon is not to be deceived by faked bleeding.' (Hynek, p. 76) (Seitz, p. 117) 'Wherever could Teresa have got so much fluid human blood?' "

This question is first fully recognized in its devastating power of proof when we pause to reckon up:

At each Passion ecstasy the loss of blood runs to at least 2 litres: the number of Passion ecstasies may be taken as 35 annually; they have been going on for 27 years already; that gives a 'consumption' or 'demand' of (35 x 27 x 2—) 1890 litres (416 gallons) of fresh, fluid blood.

"In the booklet, *Impressions of Konnersreuth,* by Cardinal and Prince-Bishop Dr. Caspar of Prague are to be found (from March 1929) numberless testimonies to the reality of the bleedings and as to the character of the blood. In the vision on the Mount of Olives (3rd vision), 'the eyes are filled with blood.' At the 5th vision, (Jesus sweats blood), 'Teresa, too, had blood running from her eyes over her cheeks.' And once more in the 5th vision 'Now the heart wound begins to bleed.' At the 7th vision 'The blood is still flowing out of her eyes.' But 'the stigma on her right hand is still dry.' Yet, at the 9th vision (the arrest), 'The wounds on her hands begin to bleed.' At the 10th vision, 'Both hands are now bleeding terribly, so that the bandage on her left one is soaked with blood. The eyes, too, are bleeding more.' He noticed too, the (apparent) contradiction in that Teresa stretches out her hands, 'although her eye-lids are so stuck together with the blood that she can see nothing.' In the 17th vision, at six o'clock on the Friday morning, he notices, 'Teresa's eyes are gummed up with blood. Down over her cheeks run two streaks of congealed blood, each two-finger breadths in width. The bed-jacket, too, is soaked with blood over her heart.' From the vision on, where Jesus takes the cross up onto His shoulders and sets out on the Way of the Cross, he notices 'Heart and hands are bleeding, and so much this time that the blood comes through her bed-jacket. Blood is running from her foot wounds, too.' When, in the 37th vision, Christ's garments are roughly stripped from Him, he sees 'fresh, red blood is now flowing from all her wounds,' Then Teresa sees Christ on the cross; 'The blood running out of her eyes has now dropped on to the front of her vest.' 'Streams of blood are meanwhile running from both the wounds on the back and palm of the right hand, uniting at the wrist. On the left, too, the bandage is already soaked with blood.'

"Professor Pabstmann, a biologist of Bamberg, assures us that many times he could observe how Teresa Neumann's crystal-clear tears changed suddenly into blood as soon as she saw in her ecstasy Christ receive the first blow from a servant of the Temple in the court of the High Priests. Pabstmann was present in 1927 at the first examination desired by the Church.

" 'On some photographs the commencement and further development of this bleeding of the eyes can be observed precisely. The blood here flows several hours, as well as thrice during the crucifixion ecstasy from the thorn stigmata, which open up at eight or nine points, mostly at the back of the head. One could preceive this quite definitely on the blood-stained shawl which Bishop Schrembs of Ohio and I handled.' (Seitz, 118 et seq.)

"All the years from 1927 to the War and since 1945, when Konnersreuth again became accessible, the bleedings have

45

been observed to be thus.

"The loss of blood in the ecstasies, especially in Lent, is considerable. Fr. Naber showed a clerical visitor a white coat which Teresa had on over two vests on Good Friday 1945; this jacket is not merely blood-stained, it is literally soaked with blood. At that time the bleeding was most copious—besides the heart wound—from the right shoulder.

"Tears of blood are nothing new in the history of Catholic mystics. They have previously been noticed in other cases, even with saints not stigmatised.

"In the case of Teresa Neumann, blood sweat often occurs, indeed regularly in the vision of the crowning with thorns about seven o'clock in the morning and at eight definite points on the skin of the head. This has hardly ever been observed in the past, only two cases having been recorded in the 19th century.

"The blood has many times been analyzed in clinical and forensic institutions. It is human blood. It consists, like any human blood, (1) of blood fluid and (2) blood corpuscles. The blood fluid (blood plasma) contains quite normally water, albumen, salt, sugar, fat; the corpuscles are in the usual proportion, red and white, and blood lamallae, iron, water and colouring matter. Generally the source of the blood samples was not disclosed to the analysts in order to make the tests as highly objective as possible. The estimated loss of blood from one Passion ecstasy varies between two and three litres; it is not always the same. Generally speaking, five litres of blood from one person is a fatal loss."

PHENOMENA IN COMMUNIONS

The first and most remarkable of these phenomena is that she not only lives but maintains a vigorous and active existence without earthly food, nourished by the Blessed Sacrament alone; and this has continued for the past thirty-one years. The most wonderful feature of this phenomenon is not that she lives without earthly food, but that the Blessed Sacrament gives her strength and vigour in a manner that is quite apparent. She herself said, in a reply to a question of Fr. Härtl, Fr. Naber's assistant, "I do not live on nothing, but on the Saviour. He said, 'My flesh is meat indeed.' Why shouldn't this be the case when He wants it to be?" As we shall see, the Sacramental Species usually remains intact in her from one Holy Communion to another, and while it remains, she has normal strength and vigour; but if, as usually happens when she is suffering for another, the Sacramental Species disappears, then she becomes weak and languid like a dying person, and regains her vigour only when she has received Holy Communion. Of this phenomenon Fr. Fahsel writes, "The phenomenal results of her receiving Holy Communion are the following:

"First a distinct strengthening of the body is immediately noticeable. She has often been found in a pitiable state of weakness before receiving, especially if one of her mystical vicarious states of suffering preceded the reception of Holy Communion. At these times her face is sunken, dark rings appear under her eyes, she can hardly sit on the chair behind the altar. All these signs of weakness disappear as soon as she has received Holy Communion."

Archbishop Teodorowicz quotes the account of Fr. Hermann Joseph, O.F.M.Cap., from the Konnersreuth Yearbook of 1929 in corroboration of the above. Fr. Hermann Joseph's account is as follows:

"I was in Konnersreuth on the twenty-fourth of May 1929, and had the good fortune of witnessing an ecstatic Communion. I was in the sacristy about to vest for Mass. Suddenly the door was opened and I beheld a countenance full of pain

47

and interior sorrow, such as I have never seen before, even in the dying. The eyes reminded me of a person parched with thirst, using up his last bit of energy to reach the fountain of water before he sinks down powerless. It was Teresa Neumann coming to receive Holy Communion . . . . When, during the Mass, the priest came to give her Holy Communion as she knelt in her place behind the altar, as soon as the Blessed Sacrament was visible, an ecstasy came upon her. She opened out both arms and stretched them towards the Sacred Host. Her eyes were not directed towards the Host, but to a Figure that I could not see. She can see the risen Saviour Himself, when I see only the veil of bread . . . . . On looking at her countenance I was forced to think of that place in Holy Writ where it says of St. Stephen: 'His face was as if it had been the face of an angel.' It was no longer the face of Teresa Neumann. It was an entirely different one showing the veneration of a creature for the greatness and majesty of its Creator." (Theodorowicz, page 316, Herder's translation).

Because of claims made, though not proved, that a few exceptional people have been found who lived for years in a natural manner without food, Benedict XIV hesitated about saying what practically all doctors now say, that such is impossible without a miracle; but, as already stated, he does say that if a person fasting from all food lives on the Blessed Sacrament alone, it is regarded as a miracle (Bk. IV, Pt. 1, Ch. 27). Catholic writers are unanimous in asserting that there are a number of well-authenticated cases of persons who have lived for several years without food or drink but who during their fast have received Holy Communion. They are to be found chiefly among the stigmatists. The following are a few of the most remarkable of these cases taken from Dr. Imbert-Goubeyre's book entitled *"La Stigmatisation"*:

Nicholas von Flú (+1487) lived for 20 years on the Blessed

Sacrament alone, which he received once a month; St. Ledwina (+1433) lived for 20 years; Venerable Dominica dal Paradiso (+1553), for 20 years; Blessed Elizabeth von Reute, for 15 years; Catherine Emmerich, for 12 years; Louise Lateau, 14 years; Teresa Neumann, for 31 years; St. Catherine of Siena, for 8 years. As to those others for whom claims have been made of their having lived in a natural manner for years without food, such as Molly Fancher, in no case have we satisfactory evidence that the fast was absolute. The only person whose case was investigated in the same was as Teresa Neumann's—the Welsh girl Sarah Jones—died after the eight day's fast from food and drink.

Two other phenomena in connection with the Blessed Sacrament, her perception of the presence of Our Saviour, and the remaining of the Sacred Species intact in her from one Holy Communion to another, may be treated together, for the fact (which people can ascertain for themselves) that she can perceive the presence or absence of the Sacred Species in others or in churches hidden from view makes it reasonable to believe that she can tell when the Sacred Species is present within herself and when the Sacramental Presence ceases. With regard to this perception of the presence of the Blessed Sacrament by stigmatized persons, Archbishop Teodorowicz writes as follows:

"The stigmatized show a special aptitude for that most exalted mystery, incomprehensible to the senses and only comprehensible through faith, the Blessed Eucharist. These souls have such a fine perception for the Holy Eucharist that they can distinguish between consecrated and unconsecrated Hosts, or recognize the place where the consecrated Host is to be found, even if this place has no distinguishing mark such as a light." On this point Görres, in his book *"Die Christliche Mystik,"* gives the following examples:

"The Cistercian nun Juliana often noticed from afar when the Blessed Sacrament was being carried away from the church at the end of religous ceremonies and was often remarked to be sad when It was taken away.

"A Carmelite monk, named Cassetus, who also had this gift of recognizing the presence of the Blessed Sacrament, was on one occasion invited by the Franciscans of Villonda to their house in order to test whether he had the gift. They removed the Blessed Sacrament to a side altar, but left the sanctuary lamp lighted before the high altar. When Cassetus arrived with a companion, he recognized immediately that the Blessed Sacrament was not at the high altar and went to the side altar though there was nothing to indicate that the Blessed Sacrament was there."

Among many others who had this gift was St. Francis Borgia, who went straight to the place in a church where the Blessed Sacrament was kept.

In the case of Teresa Neumann, it has already been mentioned under the heading of the "state of exalted rest" that, at times when, on account of illness such as happens during Lent, Holy Communion is brought to her at her house, she knows when the priest takes the Blessed Sacrament from the tabernacle and accompanies It mentally on the way to her house. If travelling in a strange country, she knows the churches in which the Blessed Sacrament is reserved even if they are not visible from the road. Fr. Wutz, who sometimes took her to Switzerland in his car, on one occasion thought that it was most unlikely that the Blessed Sacrament was reserved in a house where she had indicated Its presence. He entered the house and found that, though there was no external sign, it was a hospice for travelling priests and that the Blessed Sacrament was reserved in it.

She also perceives the presence of the Blessed Sacrament

50

in persons who have received Holy Communion, if the Sacred Species had not yet dissolved. This gift is not uncommon; there was an Irish child, known as "Little Nellie of Holy God" who could tell the Sister who had charge of her in the hospital in Cork when she had received Holy Communion and when she had not. Saint Pius X gave her a dispensation to receive Holy Communion at the age of four.

Besides Teresa's own statement that she is conscious of the continued presence of the Blessed Sacrament within her from one Holy Communion to another, corroborated by the fact that she recognizes Its presence in others, we have further evidence of this phenomenon from the fact that the Sacred Species has been found to be intact on more than one occasion when she vomited several hours after receiving. Of this phenomenon Dr. Fröhlich writes as follows:

"The Sacred Host remains wholly unconsumed within her until the hour of Holy Communion on the following day and with It, therefore, the vivifying power of Christ, who is present. This fact is incontrovertibly demonstrated by the vomiting of the gastric juice, as a consequence of mystical expiatory suffering, in which the Sacred Host was seen to be quite intact after eight, ten, and eighteen hours."

The following facts given by Fr. Fahsel illustrates what Dr. Fröhlich says about the permanence of the Sacred Species within her and throws light upon her expiatory suffering for others:

"In the month of June 1930, Teresa had taken on herself, by way of expiating suffering, the sickness of a young girl with tuberculosis who was on the point of death without any sign of sorrow for sacrileges she had committed by taking the Sacred Host out of her mouth after receiving Holy Communion, in order to make mockery of It afterwards along with some young officers. Teresa had attacks of nausea and vomit-

51

ed blood and mucus. On the evening of Saturday, July 26th, being completely exhausted, she went to bed taking with her a clean handkerchief. Scarcely was she in bed when she felt herself obliged to vomit again; to her great distress she felt that the Sacred Host, which she had received that morning, had come up into her throat and, in spite of the efforts she had made to retain It, she had to vomit It into the handkerchief she had prepared in advance.

"The Pastor, Fr. Naber, called in haste, sent for the assistant, Fr. Hártl. The latter remembered that on the evening before Teresa had said to him: 'You will have a little commotion tomorrow, but nothing will have to be burned." They did not therefore think of taking away the Sacred Species to be burned as is done in cases where It has been vomited. Teresa, holding the handkerchief extended before her, began to lament and pray: 'O gentle Saviour, behold Thou art lying there. Oh! why hast Thou gone out from me? If only I knew what I have done to Thee! I could not help it. What are we to do now?' Suddenly she sat up and assumed the usual attitude for receiving Holy Communion, at the same time falling into a state of ecstasy. The Pastor raised the handkerchief with the Sacred Host, which had remained intact, to Teresa's half-opened lips and immediately the Host disappeared from her mouth in the same mysterious manner as always happens when she is in the state of ecstasy. Teresa, falling back on her pillows murmured: 'The Saviour is again within her.' The young girl for whom Teresa had suffered died the same day, reconciled with God and fortified with the Holy Sacraments of the Church."

As already mentioned in Chapter V this extraordinary privilege was first enjoyed by Our Blessed Lady. In Vol. IV of *The City of God* (in which the revelations made to Venerable Maria d'Agreda are recorded) we read: "In this blessing the

Lord fulfilled His promise made to the Church in His Apostles, that He should be with them to the end of time (Matt. XXVIII, 20). He had already anticipated the fulfillment of this promise even at that time, when He had resolved to ascend into heaven, for He had remained sacramentally present in His Mother since the Last Supper, as related above (in Vol. iii). But it would not have been entirely fulfilled after His Ascension, if He had not wrought this new miracle in the Church; for in those first years the Apostles had no temple or proper arrangement for preserving continually the Blessed Eucharist and therefore they always consumed It entirely on the day of Its consecration. The most holy Mary alone was the sanctuary and the temple, in which for some years the most Blessed Sacrament was preserved in order that the Church of Christ might not be deprived even for one moment of the Word made flesh, from the time when He ascended into heaven until the end of the world . . ."[1]

It may be presumed that Teresa Neumann is not the only one of the stigmatists to whom this privilege of the constant presence of the Sacred Species within her has been granted, but it was enjoyed also by those others whose lives were preserved for years without the use of earthly food.

The last phenomenon in connection with her Holy Communions that we shall consider is her extraordinary hunger for the Bread of Life and the extraordinary way in which Our Divine Lord has many times satisfied that hunger, even sometimes without the ministration of a priest. F. X. Huber gives the following information on her eager desire for Holy Communion.

"She shows obvious impatience when she has to wait for Communion. Professor Wunderle asked her why Communion occasioned such a violent desire in her. She gave as answer, 'That does not arise at all from me. It is a grace.' When on

53

his way on Christmas night 1930 to give her Holy Communion, Fr. Naber dropped in to see a sick person, she grew impatient to the great astonishment of Fr. Fahsel, who sat with her and to whom she told at once the cause of the delay as well as the fact and the aim of the detour. When the reception of Holy Communion is at hand, her body comes to life, her face lights up, her eyes shine with yearning and expectation, a holy excitement comes over her and rouses her. As soon as the priest with the Blessed Sacrament approaches her, she is frequently seized with ecstasy. This is accompanied simultaneously with a vision. She raises her arms and looks in the direction of the Sacred Host in the hands of the priest. While he recites the customary prayers, she looks on with a blissful smile as if transfigured. When questioned about it she explains her peculiar behaviour thus, 'I see the Saviour as a radiant figure. Then the splendour of the figure changes to a flame of fire which comes up to me and goes into my mouth. Then I know no more, then am I wholly with the Saviour.' Interrogated about the noticeable looking up and down in the direction of the approaching priest, she affirms, 'I see the scars on the hands and feet of the Saviour, the scars on the feet I see with especially unusual radiance; and therefore she looks ever again and again downwards. At Christmas there is a childlike happiness that transfigures her face when the priest comes. Then, as she relates, the angels swoop down from heaven and, from their midst, the Christ Child steps forwards and up to her. She sees Him at about the age of two years. If she is lying in bed, she bows yearningly from her couch towards the door through which the priest has to enter; she often sees him in advance as, in the church over the way, he takes the Host from the Ciborium and comes across the village square to her parents' house, meanwhile stretching herself out of bed in a way which can no longer be reconciled with the laws of equi-

54

librium and gravity of statics and physics."

To satisfy the vehement desire for union with Our Lord in the Blessed Sacrament, at times the Host is received without any motion of swallowing; at others, It leaves the priest's fingers and comes to her; and, finally, there are times when Holy Communion comes to her without the ministry of the priest. On these points we quote again from F. X. Huber:

"Cardinal Caspar (who gave her Holy Communion several times) made careful observations of the manner in which she receives Holy Communion, and writes:

"Teresa made not the slightest movement and there was not the faintest attempt at swallowing . . . . . The Sacred Host was no longer visible. It vanished entirely of Its own accord, just as Bishop Dr. Waitz and others had already witnessed.' (cf. Gerlich I, 167; Seitz, 159; Fahsel, 86). In order to convince himself of the fact, Gerlich placed himself so near that he could see as far as the back of the tongue and the gums of the opened mouth. 'From the first opening of her mouth Teresa made no movement of swallowing. Suddenly the Host disappeared.' On the same occasion the Capuchin Father, Hermann Josephus of Kempton, a pace behind him sideways, had observed every one of her movements closely so as to go away satisfied. The Sacred Host vanished when the priest had hardly placed It on her tongue, at once, without staying in the mouth. Further observations of the gliding of the Host were demonstrated and verified; often the Host slipped from the hand of the approaching priest and glided free to the opened mouth of Teresa. The first persons to see this, before they believed, were under the impression that they were the victims of self-illusion. Renewed observations confirmed the fact —a camera cannot have illusions—and photographs show without a doubt the Host floating from between the fingers of the priest on the way to her. Priests who have administered Communion to her while on a visit to Konnersreuth, Eichstätt, or elsewhere, have experienced this many times and—astounded—have seen lying right on the tongue the Host which they have just been holding in their fingers, for it only to vanish at once."

On her reception of the Blessed Sacrament without the ministration of a priest we quote the following cases from Dr. de Poray Madeyski's book:

"A third way in which she received Holy Communion, according to eye-witnesses, is without the co-operation of the priest. Thus, for example, when she and her sister were staying at the house of Professor Wutz at Eichstätt (where she has often spent periods of a month to six weeks), on the night of the 29th April, 1929, she was enduring great sufferings which increased to such a degree that some priests who were present were thinking of bringing her Holy Communion from the tabernacle in the private oratory of the house where a consecrated Host had been reserved for her Communion of the following day. Suddenly they saw her sit up in the attitude which she assumes for the reception of Holy Communion. She passed immediately into a state of ecstasy and said, 'She has received the Saviour; go and see; He has disappeared from the tabernacle.' The Priest went and found that the Host that had been reserved was no longer there.

"Another day Fr. Fahsel perceived that at the moment when he was about to give her Holy Communion she had already the Sacred Host in her mouth. Having entered into a state of ecstasy immediately, she called him back to explain the fact to him. She said, 'Teresa was very weak and desired the Saviour eagerly. There were two wicked men outside who had just mocked the Saviour. Teresa knew it and her desire became still more ardent. It is for that reason that He has come to her sooner.'"

We take the following additional cases of Teresa's receiving Holy Communion without the ministration of a priest from Archbishop Teodorowicz's *"Mystical Phenomena of Teresa Neumann"*:

"An eye-witness described to me the following incident. Teresa was staying in his home . . . . . and while there undertook expiatory sufferings (with the permission of the Saviour) for the dying mother of a well-known scholar. Her physical and spiritual sufferings were terrible. But how great was his surprise when Teresa suddenly in an ecstasy opened her mouth, her hands folded on her breast, then closed her mouth and bowed her head just like someone who had received Holy Communion. The surprise and shock of the one who is my authority, in this affair the head of the house where she stayed, reached its height when he found that the consecrated Host that had been intended for Teresa was missing in the house chapel. The same witness told me a similar, if not more surprising case. Teresa was in Konnersreuth, several hours by rail distant from the place where he was. One day when the Pastor brought her Holy Communion, she was already in the state in which she usually is after Communion. She told him without any further explanation that she had already received on that day. In the meantime, the priest who told me of the incident noted that on the same day at the same hour one of the three consecrated Hosts which he had reserved in his private chapel had disappeared."

The Archbishop gives a third case of which the Pastor and Fr. Fahsel were witnesses. Teresa came to the Presbytery at half-past ten in the morning, and asked for Holy Communion. She was given the key of the Sacristy, but was so weak that she was not able to open the door. It was learned that she had been suffering for a dying person. When the door was opened for her, she struggled into her place behind the altar.

The Pastor asked Fr. Fahsel to give her Holy Communion. When he went round to where she was kneeling, after the usual prayers had been recited, he found that she had already received Holy Communion.

These cases where she has received Holy Communion without the ministration of a priest have given some people trouble. They say that the priest is the person appointed by God to give Holy Communion; that there is reason therefore for suspicion if a person seems to receive Holy Communion without him. Besides, they say cases of fraud have been discovered.

Let us take the last case first. Why had she not attended morning Mass and received Holy Communion at it? The answer to that question is simple. She had been suffering for a dying person, and when she suffers for a sick person, she feels the weakness of the sick person. In the case we are considering the person was dying. She was, therefore, unable to go to Mass at the ordinary time, and went for Holy Communion when a little strength returned. When she suffers for the conversion of someone, the Sacred Species dissolves a couple of hours before her next Communion; hence, the great weakness. For the past thirty-one years the whole period of Lent has every year been a time of great suffering when she is physically unable to go to Mass.

With regard to the larger question, the receiving of Holy Communion without the ministration of a priest, it is true that a few cases of fraud have been discovered; but the very fact that a few misguided persons have resorted to fraud in this matter in order to gain a reputation for holiness is an indication that there have been well-authenticated cases of people reputed to be holy who have received Communion without the ministration of a priest.

The late Fr. Thurston, S.J., devotes a chapter of his *"Physi-*

cal Phenomena of Mysticism" to this question. While he admits that there have been a few cases of fraud, he regards it as quite certain that there have been many well-authenticated cases of holy people whose great hunger for the Bread of Life has been satisfied by Our Lord Himself or by the ministration of an angel, even in cases like the last-mentioned one in connection with Teresa Neumann, when a priest was present who could have given Holy Communion. In this chapter, Fr. Thurston gives seven cases, two of which were cases where the Host left the fingers of the priests giving Holy Communion and went to the person receiving; the other five cases were ones in which the Blessed Sacrament either left the altar while the priest was saying Mass or came from a distance.

The six cases given by Fr. Thurston are as follows:

The first case happened to St. John Vianney, the Curé of Ars. In one of his catechetical instructions, he said that a certain person had doubted about the Real Presence and prayed to the Blessed Virgin to obtain for him the gift of faith. When he, the Curé of Ars, was about to give Holy Communion to this man, the Sacred Host detached Itself from his fingers when he was still a good distance from him, and placed Itself on his tongue.

The second case occurred to the saintly Fr. Olier, the Founder of St. Sulpice. He relates that when he was giving Holy Communion to the Nuns of a certain community, the Sacred Host detached Itself from his fingers and placed Itself on the tongue of one of the Sisters, whom he afterwards identified. Another priest had a similar experience with the same Sister; he said that he had seen the Sacred Host fly out of his hand into her mouth.

Of those who have received Holy Communion without the ministration of a priest, the first case mentioned by Fr. Thurston is that of the Dominican Sister, Mother Agnes of

Jesus. According to her own account, she frequently received Holy Communion from the hands of angels or from the Blessed in heaven. On one occasion the chaplain, Fr. Martinon, refused to allow her to receive Holy Communion at his Mass. He learned afterwards that an angel gave her Communion, whereupon he examined the Ciborium in which he had left four hosts, and found that one of them was missing.

A third well-known case is that of St. Catherine of Siena. It was a frequent occurrence for the Blessed Sacrament to leave the priest's fingers and go into her mouth. This is vouched for by Blessed Raymund of Capua, her confessor, who was afterwards General of the Dominicans, and by several others. On two occasions, while he was saying Mass, a particle of the Sacred Host left the altar and was received by St. Catherine. On the second of these occasions he was much troubled, for he thought that the particle had fallen on the ground. St. Catherine, when questioned confessed that Our Lord Himself deigned to bring the particle to her and give her Holy Communion with His own sacred hands.

A fourth case is that of Blessed Elizabeth von Reute. Her confessor, who wrote an account of her life soon after her death, says in it that on one occasion, as he was bringing Holy Communion to her sick room preceded by an acolyte, the particle intended for her left the paten, and when, after a fruitless search, he went to her cell, he found her in an ecstasy. She comforted him and assured him that the particle was not lost as he feared, but that Our Lord Himself, preceded by an angel, came and gave her Communion with His own hand.

A fifth case is that of Venerable Dominica dal Paradiso (who lived for twenty years without earthly food). Her confessor, Fr. Francisco Onesti, had prayed to God to give him a sign by which he might know whether the wonderful things related about Sister Dominica were from Him; and he asked as a sign that an angel should bring her Holy Communion from the altar while he said Mass. After months of prayer and holy fear lest he might be guilty of presumption in asking for such a sign, on a Holy Saturday an invisible hand took away a particle of the Host from the altar. He feared it had been lost, but after Mass he remembered his petition for a sign and went to Sister Dominica. She told him that the particle had been brought to her by her Angel Guardian at the very time he was saying Mass.

The sixth case is that of St. Maria Francesca of the Five Wounds (whose stigmata resemble those of Fr. Pio of our own time). It is recorded in her life and is well authenticated that she more than once not only received Holy Communion by the ministration of an angel while Mass was going on, but that she received the chalice also. The Archangel Raphael took the chalice from the altar after the consecration on more than one occasion, and allowed her to drink from it. A similar case of reception of Holy Communion under both species is recorded in the life of Sister Mary of the Passion, an Italian Sister who died in 1912.

In this connection readers will recall how the three children of Fatima received Holy Communion from the hands of the angel who had been sent to them to prepare them for Our Lady's visit. The angel, who said that he was the Angel of Peace and the Guardian Angel of Portugal, appeared to them with a chalice in his hand and holding a Host over it. Blood from the Host dripped into the chalice. The angel gave the Host to Lucia, who had made her First Communion, and the contents of the chalice to Francisco and Jacinta, who had not. Judging from the case quoted above, we may presume that the angel took the consecrated Host with the permission of Our Lord from some church.

Returning to Teresa Neumann, it has been admitted by all,

even by the greatest sceptics, with possibly one exception, that in her case fraud must be ruled out completely as the explanation of any of the phenomena connected with her. In the case of her Holy Communions it would be absolutely impossible; there are more credible witnesses of the extraordinary circumstances of her Holy Communions than in any of the other cases we have mentioned. Such phenomena, we may safely presume, are permitted to happen by Almighty God, not only to satisfy the spiritual hunger for the Bread of Life of these devout souls, but to strengthen the faith of others and increase their devotion to the Blessed Sacrament. It is, alas! too true that many Catholics receive Holy Communion only at long intervals and with reluctance, that the number who visit Our Lord in the tabernacle outside the times when they are obliged by precept to attend Mass is small, and that the number of those who are willing to watch with Him for a Holy Hour is smaller still.

As price of her great privilege of having the Sacred Species within her for the whole day, Teresa Neumann watches with Him day and night without food or sleep. She is always conscious of His Divine Presence, and is therefore always cheerful and affable even in the midst of her greatest sufferings. She herself has remarked that she dare not be otherwise when she knows that the Blessed Saviour is present within her. If anyone, therefore, is inclined to cavil at the marvellous ways in which her desire for Holy Communion is satisfied, let him ask which is the greater wonder: that Our Lord should come from a distant tabernacle to satisfy the desire of a person who lives on Him alone, or that He should come at all to a person of little faith who receives Him without preparation and goes away immediately and becomes immersed in the things of this world just as if he had received mere ordinary bread?